GET COACHED UP

BY COACH TRAVIS JOHNSON

Copyright © 2024 by Travis Johnson.

Produced for Publication by The Author's Pen, LLC
PO Box 16314
Fort Worth, Texas 76162
www.tapwriting.com

ALL RIGHTS ARE RESERVED.

No part of this publication may be reproduced, stored in a retrieval system, or transmitted, in any form or by any means, electronic, mechanical, photocopying, recording or otherwise, without the prior written permission of the publisher.

Get Coached Up.
1st paperback ed. ISBN 978-1-948-248-55-6

COACHTRAVISJOHNSON

THIS JOURNAL BELONGS TO:

_____

THIS POCKET JOURNAL/QUOTE MOTIVATOR GUARANTEES TO CHALLENGE AND INSPIRE YOU TO BECOME A BETTER VERSION OF YOURSELF, EMPOWERING YOU TO COMPLETE MORE PERSONAL TASKS AND ACCOMPLISH MORE PROFESSIONAL GOALS IN YOUR LIFETIME.

LET'S GO!!!

TABLE OF CONTENTS

Get to Know Coach 5

Introduction 7

Coach's 4 Easy Steps To Journaling 8

Self Motivation Quotes 9

Spiritual Quotes 41

Sports Quotes 73

Leadership & Business Quotes....................95

GET TO KNOW COACH

For over 30 years, Coach Johnson has been an inspirational leader as a business owner, corporate executive, head coach, supervisor, team captain, and mentor. He has reached enormous levels of success by applying his motto, "Win Lives, Win Games" to everything he does. His motto stems from the principles of having PASSION, PURPOSE, and choosing PERSPECTIVE as a position to guide him. This has resulted in countless victories and success stories over his years as a coach, mentor, and speaker. Using each experience as an opportunity, Coach uses positive energy, a positive attitude, discipline, versatility, straightforward and real-talk communication approach, to relate with everyone. As a result, he is sought after across the globe by industry leaders, schools, teams, companies, and organizations.

For the work and goals he has achieved, he is widely considered *The People's Coach*, and is committed to fulfilling his mission of creating a legacy of inspiring others to achieve more of their life goals, also empowering them to become the best version of themselves and have a positive impact on the world.

LET'S GO!!!

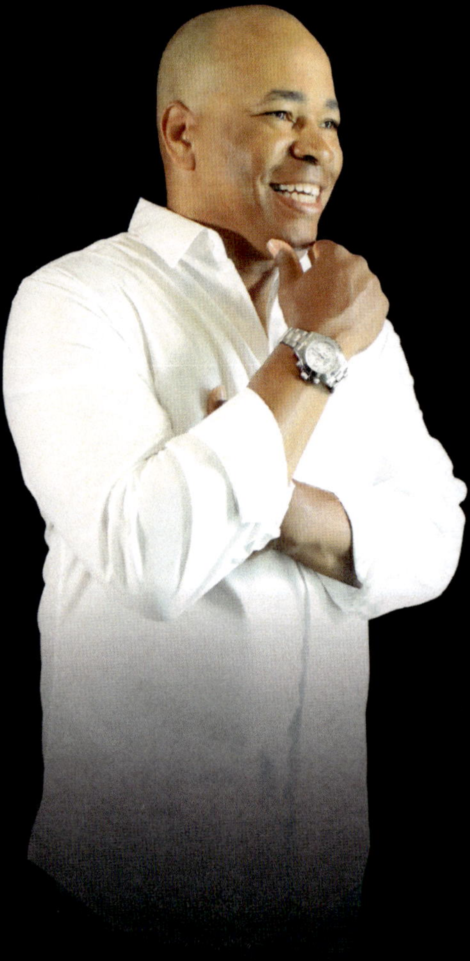

INTRODUCTION

Welcome to the "Get Coached Up" Pocket Journal/Quote Motivator by Coach Travis Johnson.

Thank you for allowing me to join you on your life journey and for enabling me to use my principles of PASSION, PURPOSE, and PERSPECTIVE to empower you to become the best version of yourself.

This self-guided pocket journal/quote motivator is guaranteed to inspire you to creatively think, organize and plan ideas, document action steps for accountability, and develop disciplined habits with work ethic to achieve personal and professional life goals.

With continued use of this motivational tool, you will not only accomplish more goals but also benefit from improved perception, concentration, memory, and information processing skills, improving your overall mental well-being through the exercise of journaling.

You are your own best guide. Open these pages to reflect, dream, and be challenged. As you add vision & drive while accessing the wisdom and inspiration already inside of you, everything will be possible on your journey ahead.

Get ready to be inspired to achieve more daily.

LET'S GO!!!

COACH'S 4 EASY STEPS TO JOURNALING

1. Schedule time to write daily.
2. Make it easy. Keep a pen and your journal with you at all times so you are ready when your thoughts begin to activate.
3. Write what you feel. Your journal does not have to follow any structure unless you want it to.
4. You don't have to share your journal notes. They are personal and designed to organize your thoughts and motivate you.

Remember to be good to yourself and take care of your mind-health. Enjoy the exercise of journaling and the benefits it will have on your mental well-being. Win your thinking and writing by journaling daily!

Furthermore, every page in the CTJ Pocket Journal/Quote Motivator will purposely prompt you to answer repetitive, self-guided questions in addition to providing you with motivational quotes to inspire you to think more critically. This method will help in exploring what you will do, when you will do it, how you will do it, and why you will do it. As a result of this journaling approach, you will become *more* motivated, you will establish clear goals *more* quickly, you will complete *more* personal tasks, and achieve more professional goals throughout your life.

LET'S GO!!!

SELF MOTIVATION QUOTES

WHAT I WILL DO?

_____
_____
_____
_____
_____

WHEN I WILL DO IT?

_____
_____
_____
_____
_____

HOW I WILL DO IT?

_____
_____
_____
_____
_____

WHY I WILL DO IT?

_____
_____
_____
_____
_____

LET'S GO!!!

I WANT TO BE THE REASON YOU DON'T QUIT

WHAT I WILL DO?

_____
_____
_____
_____

WHEN I WILL DO IT?

_____
_____
_____
_____

HOW I WILL DO IT?

_____
_____
_____
_____

WHY I WILL DO IT?

_____
_____
_____
_____

LET'S GO!!!

DON'T MAKE THE MISTAKE OF THINKING YOU HAVE TIME
DO IT NOW

WHAT I WILL DO?

_____
_____
_____
_____
_____

WHEN I WILL DO IT?

_____
_____
_____
_____
_____

HOW I WILL DO IT?

_____
_____
_____
_____
_____

WHY I WILL DO IT?

_____
_____
_____
_____
_____

LET'S GO!!!

**LIFE BECOMES LIMITLESS
WHEN YOU LIMIT WHO
HAS ACCESS TO YOU**

WHAT I WILL DO?

_____
_____
_____
_____

WHEN I WILL DO IT?

_____
_____
_____
_____

HOW I WILL DO IT?

_____
_____
_____
_____

WHY I WILL DO IT?

_____
_____
_____
_____

LET'S GO!!!

YOU BECOME YOUR THOUGHTS

WHAT I WILL DO?

_____
_____
_____
_____
_____

WHEN I WILL DO IT?

_____
_____
_____
_____
_____

HOW I WILL DO IT?

_____
_____
_____
_____
_____

WHY I WILL DO IT?

_____
_____
_____
_____
_____

LET'S GO!!!

**DREAMS BECOME REALITY
WHEN YOUR THOUGHTS
BECOME ACTION**

WHAT I WILL DO?

_____
_____
_____
_____
_____

WHEN I WILL DO IT?

_____
_____
_____
_____
_____

HOW I WILL DO IT?

_____
_____
_____
_____
_____

WHY I WILL DO IT?

_____
_____
_____
_____
_____

LET'S GO!!!

WIN YOUR PROCESS
TO WIN YOUR RESULTS

WHAT I WILL DO?

_____
_____
_____
_____
_____

WHEN I WILL DO IT?

_____
_____
_____
_____
_____

HOW I WILL DO IT?

_____
_____
_____
_____
_____

WHY I WILL DO IT?

_____
_____
_____
_____
_____

LET'S GO!!!

IF YOU WANT DIFFERENT YOU MUST MOVE DIFFERENT

WHAT I WILL DO?

_____
_____
_____
_____

WHEN I WILL DO IT?

_____
_____
_____
_____

HOW I WILL DO IT?

_____
_____
_____
_____

WHY I WILL DO IT?

_____
_____
_____
_____

LET'S GO!!!

SUCCESS
IS MOTIVATED BY FAILURE

WHAT I WILL DO?

_____
_____
_____
_____

WHEN I WILL DO IT?

_____
_____
_____
_____

HOW I WILL DO IT?

_____
_____
_____
_____

WHY I WILL DO IT?

_____
_____
_____
_____

LET'S GO!!!

WORK HARD IN SILENCE
LET YOUR WINNING
BE YOUR NOISE

WHAT I WILL DO?

_____
_____
_____
_____
_____

WHEN I WILL DO IT?

_____
_____
_____
_____
_____

HOW I WILL DO IT?

_____
_____
_____
_____
_____

WHY I WILL DO IT?

_____
_____
_____
_____
_____

LET'S GO!!!

DREAM BIG ENOUGH
SO OTHERS ARE IMPACTED
WHEN IT'S ACHIEVED

WHAT I WILL DO?

_____
_____
_____
_____

WHEN I WILL DO IT?

_____
_____
_____
_____

HOW I WILL DO IT?

_____
_____
_____
_____

WHY I WILL DO IT?

_____
_____
_____
_____

LET'S GO!!!

IT'S A FULL TIME JOB BELIEVING IN YOURSELF
NO DAYS OFF

WHAT I WILL DO?

_____
_____
_____
_____

WHEN I WILL DO IT?

_____
_____
_____
_____

HOW I WILL DO IT?

_____
_____
_____
_____

WHY I WILL DO IT?

_____
_____
_____
_____

LET'S GO!!!

**TO BE THE BEST
IT TAKES
WHAT IT TAKES**

WHAT I WILL DO?

_____
_____
_____
_____
_____

WHEN I WILL DO IT?

_____
_____
_____
_____

HOW I WILL DO IT?

_____
_____
_____
_____

WHY I WILL DO IT?

_____
_____
_____
_____

LET'S GO!!!

ALWAYS HAVE AN ATTITUDE OF GRATITUDE

WHAT I WILL DO?

_____
_____
_____
_____
_____

WHEN I WILL DO IT?

_____
_____
_____
_____
_____

HOW I WILL DO IT?

_____
_____
_____
_____
_____

WHY I WILL DO IT?

_____
_____
_____
_____
_____

LET'S GO!!!

MOTIVATED IS A LIFESTYLE

WHAT I WILL DO?

_____
_____
_____
_____

WHEN I WILL DO IT?

_____
_____
_____
_____

HOW I WILL DO IT?

_____
_____
_____
_____

WHY I WILL DO IT?

_____
_____
_____
_____

LET'S GO!!!

I WANT TO BE
THE REASON YOU BECOME
THE BEST VERSION
OF YOURSELF

SPIRITUAL QUOTES

WHAT I WILL DO?

_____
_____
_____
_____

WHEN I WILL DO IT?

_____
_____
_____
_____

HOW I WILL DO IT?

_____
_____
_____
_____

WHY I WILL DO IT?

_____
_____
_____
_____

LET'S GO!!!

GOD'S TIMING
IS PERFECT

WHAT I WILL DO?

_____
_____
_____
_____
_____

WHEN I WILL DO IT?

_____
_____
_____
_____

HOW I WILL DO IT?

_____
_____
_____
_____

WHY I WILL DO IT?

_____
_____
_____
_____
_____

LET'S GO!!!

NEW DAY
NEW THOUGHTS
NEW PRAYERS
NEW BLESSINGS

WHAT I WILL DO?

_____
_____
_____
_____

WHEN I WILL DO IT?

_____
_____
_____
_____

HOW I WILL DO IT?

_____
_____
_____
_____

WHY I WILL DO IT?

_____
_____
_____
_____

LET'S GO!!!

DON'T BE THE WEAPON FORMED AGAINST YOU KEEPING YOU FROM PROSPERING

WHAT I WILL DO?

_____
_____
_____
_____

WHEN I WILL DO IT?

_____
_____
_____
_____

HOW I WILL DO IT?

_____
_____
_____
_____

WHY I WILL DO IT?

_____
_____
_____
_____

LET'S GO!!!

MOVE WITH GODFIDENCE

WHAT I WILL DO?

_____
_____
_____
_____

WHEN I WILL DO IT?

_____
_____
_____
_____

HOW I WILL DO IT?

_____
_____
_____
_____

WHY I WILL DO IT?

_____
_____
_____
_____

LET'S GO!!!

YOUR MOUTH CAN
BLOCK YOUR BLESSINGS
KNOW WHEN TO BE QUIET

WHAT I WILL DO?

_____
_____
_____
_____

WHEN I WILL DO IT?

_____
_____
_____
_____

HOW I WILL DO IT?

_____
_____
_____
_____

WHY I WILL DO IT?

_____
_____
_____
_____

LET'S GO!!!

GIVE MORE
THAN YOU GET AND GOD WILL BLESS YOU WITH MORE THAN YOU EVER DREAMED

WHAT I WILL DO?

_____
_____
_____
_____

WHEN I WILL DO IT?

_____
_____
_____
_____

HOW I WILL DO IT?

_____
_____
_____
_____

WHY I WILL DO IT?

_____
_____
_____
_____

LET'S GO!!!

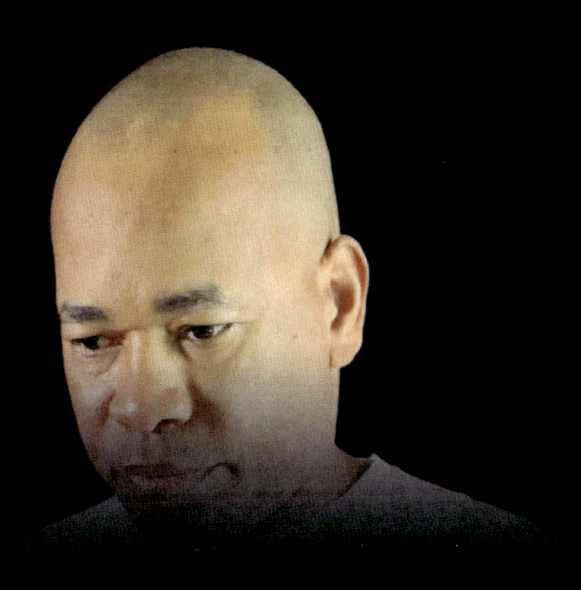

IT'S A BLESSING
TO HANDLE WHAT YOU THOUGHT WOULD HANDLE YOU

WHAT I WILL DO?

_____
_____
_____
_____

WHEN I WILL DO IT?

_____
_____
_____
_____

HOW I WILL DO IT?

_____
_____
_____
_____

WHY I WILL DO IT?

_____
_____
_____
_____

LET'S GO!!!

WHAT DIDN'T WORK OUT FOR YOU REALLY WORKED OUT FOR YOU

WHAT I WILL DO?

_____
_____
_____
_____

WHEN I WILL DO IT?

_____
_____
_____
_____

HOW I WILL DO IT?

_____
_____
_____
_____

WHY I WILL DO IT?

_____
_____
_____
_____

LET'S GO!!!

EVERYONE IS NOT EQUIPPED TO HANDLE THE ALTITUDE WHERE GOD IS TAKING YOU

WHAT I WILL DO?

_____
_____
_____
_____
_____

WHEN I WILL DO IT?

_____
_____
_____
_____

HOW I WILL DO IT?

_____
_____
_____
_____

WHY I WILL DO IT?

_____
_____
_____
_____
_____

LET'S GO!!!

WHEN GOD IS DOING SOMETHING IN YOUR LIFE YOU CAN'T SEE IT'S BECAUSE HE IS DOING SOMETHING YOU JUST CAN'T SEE

WHAT I WILL DO?

_____
_____
_____
_____
_____

WHEN I WILL DO IT?

_____
_____
_____
_____
_____

HOW I WILL DO IT?

_____
_____
_____
_____
_____

WHY I WILL DO IT?

_____
_____
_____
_____
_____

LET'S GO!!!

YOUR GIFT WILL MAKE ROOM FOR YOU

WHAT I WILL DO?

_____
_____
_____
_____

WHEN I WILL DO IT?

_____
_____
_____
_____

HOW I WILL DO IT?

_____
_____
_____
_____

WHY I WILL DO IT?

_____
_____
_____
_____
_____

LET'S GO!!!

GOD REMOVES PEOPLE FROM YOUR LIFE BECAUSE HE HEARD A CONVERSATION YOU DIDN'T HEAR

WHAT I WILL DO?

_____
_____
_____
_____

WHEN I WILL DO IT?

_____
_____
_____
_____

HOW I WILL DO IT?

_____
_____
_____
_____

WHY I WILL DO IT?

_____
_____
_____
_____
_____

LET'S GO!!!

DO YOUR PART AND GOD WILL DO THE REST

WHAT I WILL DO?

_____
_____
_____
_____

WHEN I WILL DO IT?

_____
_____
_____
_____

HOW I WILL DO IT?

_____
_____
_____
_____

WHY I WILL DO IT?

_____
_____
_____
_____

LET'S GO!!!

TRUST GOD
TO DO IT FOR YOU

WHAT I WILL DO?

_____
_____
_____
_____
_____

WHEN I WILL DO IT?

_____
_____
_____
_____
_____

HOW I WILL DO IT?

_____
_____
_____
_____

WHY I WILL DO IT?

_____
_____
_____
_____
_____

LET'S GO!!!

ONE DAY YOU WILL BE THANKFUL THAT IT WENT GOD'S WAY

SPORTS QUOTES

WHAT I WILL DO?

_____
_____
_____
_____

WHEN I WILL DO IT?

_____
_____
_____
_____

HOW I WILL DO IT?

_____
_____
_____
_____

WHY I WILL DO IT?

_____
_____
_____
_____

LET'S GO!!!

ADVERSITY & OPPORTUNITY
REVEALS CHARACTER

WHAT I WILL DO?

_____
_____
_____
_____

WHEN I WILL DO IT?

_____
_____
_____
_____

HOW I WILL DO IT?

_____
_____
_____
_____

WHY I WILL DO IT?

_____
_____
_____
_____

LET'S GO!!!

SUCCESS REQUIRES SACRIFICE

WHAT I WILL DO?

_____
_____
_____
_____
_____

WHEN I WILL DO IT?

_____
_____
_____
_____
_____

HOW I WILL DO IT?

_____
_____
_____
_____

WHY I WILL DO IT?

_____
_____
_____
_____
_____

LET'S GO!!!

WINNING IS A LIFESTYLE

WHAT I WILL DO?

_____
_____
_____
_____

WHEN I WILL DO IT?

_____
_____
_____
_____

HOW I WILL DO IT?

_____
_____
_____
_____

WHY I WILL DO IT?

_____
_____
_____
_____

LET'S GO!!!

PRACTICE WITH PURPOSE

WHAT I WILL DO?

_____
_____
_____
_____

WHEN I WILL DO IT?

_____
_____
_____
_____

HOW I WILL DO IT?

_____
_____
_____
_____

WHY I WILL DO IT?

_____
_____
_____
_____

LET'S GO!!!

WIN LIVES
WIN GAMES

WHAT I WILL DO?

_____
_____
_____
_____
_____

WHEN I WILL DO IT?

_____
_____
_____
_____
_____

HOW I WILL DO IT?

_____
_____
_____
_____
_____

WHY I WILL DO IT?

_____
_____
_____
_____
_____

LET'S GO!!!

DISCIPLINE IS DOING SOMETHING YOU HATE LIKE YOU LOVE IT

WHAT I WILL DO?

_____
_____
_____
_____

WHEN I WILL DO IT?

_____
_____
_____
_____

HOW I WILL DO IT?

_____
_____
_____
_____

WHY I WILL DO IT?

_____
_____
_____
_____

LET'S GO!!!

GREAT TO DEVELOP GOOD PLAYERS GREATER TO DEVELOP GOOD PEOPLE

WHAT I WILL DO?

_____
_____
_____
_____

WHEN I WILL DO IT?

_____
_____
_____
_____

HOW I WILL DO IT?

_____
_____
_____
_____

WHY I WILL DO IT?

_____
_____
_____
_____
_____

LET'S GO!!!

**BEFORE EVERY SUCCESS
THERE IS A PROCESS
THAT GIVES YOU NO CHOICE
BUT TO WIN**

WHAT I WILL DO?

_____
_____
_____
_____
_____

WHEN I WILL DO IT?

_____
_____
_____
_____
_____

HOW I WILL DO IT?

_____
_____
_____
_____

WHY I WILL DO IT?

_____
_____
_____
_____
_____

LET'S GO!!!

DISCIPLINE
CREATES DOMINANCE

WHAT I WILL DO?

_____
_____
_____
_____
_____

WHEN I WILL DO IT?

_____
_____
_____
_____
_____

HOW I WILL DO IT?

_____
_____
_____
_____
_____

WHY I WILL DO IT?

_____
_____
_____
_____
_____

LET'S GO!!!

**BE URGENT & RELENTLESS
IN YOUR PROCESS
AND YOU WILL IMPOSE
ON A SUCCESSFUL RESULT**

LEADERSHIP & BUSINESS QUOTES

WHAT I WILL DO?

_____
_____
_____
_____
_____

WHEN I WILL DO IT?

_____
_____
_____
_____
_____

HOW I WILL DO IT?

_____
_____
_____
_____
_____

WHY I WILL DO IT?

_____
_____
_____
_____
_____

LET'S GO!!!

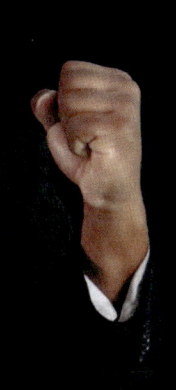

LEAD WITH LOVE

WHAT I WILL DO?

_____
_____
_____
_____

WHEN I WILL DO IT?

_____
_____
_____
_____

HOW I WILL DO IT?

_____
_____
_____
_____

WHY I WILL DO IT?

_____
_____
_____
_____

LET'S GO!!!

BLESSED IS THE LEADER
WHO SEEKS THE BEST
FOR WHOM THEY LEAD

WHAT I WILL DO?

_____
_____
_____
_____

WHEN I WILL DO IT?

_____
_____
_____
_____

HOW I WILL DO IT?

_____
_____
_____
_____

WHY I WILL DO IT?

_____
_____
_____
_____
_____

LET'S GO!!!

PROCRASTINATION
IS THE ENEMY OF EXECUTION

WHAT I WILL DO?

_____
_____
_____
_____
_____

WHEN I WILL DO IT?

_____
_____
_____
_____
_____

HOW I WILL DO IT?

_____
_____
_____
_____

WHY I WILL DO IT?

_____
_____
_____
_____
_____

LET'S GO!!!

DON'T ASPIRE TO MAKE A LIVING ASPIRE TO MAKE A DIFFERENCE

WHAT I WILL DO?

WHEN I WILL DO IT?

HOW I WILL DO IT?

WHY I WILL DO IT?

LET'S GO!!!

**IF YOU TALK THE TALK
THEN WALK THE WALK
OR JUST STOP
TALKING**

WHAT I WILL DO?
___
___
___
___
___

WHEN I WILL DO IT?
___
___
___
___
___

HOW I WILL DO IT?
___
___
___
___
___

WHY I WILL DO IT?
___
___
___
___
___

LET'S GO!!!

CONSISTENCY
EARNS CURRENCY

WHAT I WILL DO?

_____
_____
_____
_____

WHEN I WILL DO IT?

_____
_____
_____
_____

HOW I WILL DO IT?

_____
_____
_____
_____

WHY I WILL DO IT?

_____
_____
_____
_____

LET'S GO!!!

PERSPECTIVE
DRIVES PERFORMANCE

WHAT I WILL DO?

_____
_____
_____
_____
_____

WHEN I WILL DO IT?

_____
_____
_____
_____
_____

HOW I WILL DO IT?

_____
_____
_____
_____
_____

WHY I WILL DO IT?

_____
_____
_____
_____
_____

LET'S GO!!!

**BE LIMITLESS & FEARLESS
IN YOUR THOUGHT PROCESS
& YOU WILL BE LIMITLESS IN
YOUR INCOME
& LIFE OPPORTUNITIES**

WHAT I WILL DO?

_____
_____
_____
_____

WHEN I WILL DO IT?

_____
_____
_____
_____

HOW I WILL DO IT?

_____
_____
_____
_____

WHY I WILL DO IT?

_____
_____
_____
_____
_____

LET'S GO!!!

STANDARDS
WILL ELIMINATE
PRETENDERS

WHAT I WILL DO?

_____
_____
_____
_____
_____

WHEN I WILL DO IT?

_____
_____
_____
_____
_____

HOW I WILL DO IT?

_____
_____
_____
_____

WHY I WILL DO IT?

_____
_____
_____
_____
_____

LET'S GO!!!

IF YOU DON'T SEE WORK AS AN OPPORTUNITY THEN YOUR VISION OF SUCCESS WILL HAVE LIMITATIONS